Test Your IQ

Philip Carter and Ken Russell

foulsham
LONDON • NEW YORK • TORONTO • SYDNEY

foulsham

The Publishing House, Bennetts Close, Cippenham,
Slough, Berkshire, SL1 5AP, England

ISBN 0-572-02484-3

Copyright © 1999 Philip Carter and Ken Russell

Cover photograph © Rob Colvin/SIS Ltd.

Printed in Great Britain by Cox & Wyman Ltd., Reading, Berks.

Contents

Introduction   7
  About the authors   7
  What is IQ?   7

How to use this book   10

Test 1   11
  Answers and scoring chart   24

Test 2   29
  Answers and scoring chart   42

Test 3   48
  Answers and scoring chart   62

Test 4   67
  Answers and scoring chart   80

Test 5   86
  Answers and scoring chart   98

Test 6   104
  Answers and scoring chart   116

Test 7   122
  Answers and scoring chart   134

Test 8   140
  Answers and scoring chart   152

Total scoring chart for the eight tests   158

Introduction

About the Authors

Ken Russell is a London surveyor and is Puzzle Editor of the *British Mensa Magazine*, a magazine which is sent to its 40 000 British members monthly.

Philip Carter is a JP and an Estimator from Yorkshire. He is Puzzle Editor of *Enigmasig*, the monthly newsletter of the Mensa Puzzle Special Interests group.

What is IQ?

IQ is the abbreviation for Intelligence Quotient. The dictionary definition of quotient is 'the number of times one quantity is contained within another'. The definition of intelligence is 'intellectual skill', 'mental brightness', 'quick of mind'.

When measuring the IQ of a child, the child would attempt an intelligence test which had been given to thousands of children, and the results correlated so that the average score had been assessed for each age group. Thus, a child who at eight years of age obtained a result expected of a ten-year-old, would score an IQ of 125 by the following simple calculation:

$$\frac{\text{Mental age}}{\text{Chronological age}} \times 100 = \text{IQ}$$

$$\therefore \frac{10}{8} \times 100 = 125 \text{ IQ}$$

This does not apply to adults, whose assessment would be based on results correlated to known percentages of the population.

A child with a high IQ would have a great advantage at school with his or her studies, as understanding of lessons would be easily absorbed, but, in itself, a high IQ is not a key to success in later life. More important would be the qualities of competitiveness, personality, ambition, determination and temperament. In most walks of life, however, problem-solving is encountered and a person with an high IQ is therefore well adapted to be successful in this field.

The average IQ is, obviously, 100. The population can be split roughly into three groups: 50 per cent would be between 90 and 110, 25 per cent would be above 110 and 25 per cent would be below 90.

Until recently, Intelligence Tests have been mainly related to knowledge of words, but with the advent of the increasing larger proportion of immigrants to Britain, whose knowledge of English would not be expected to be of a high standard, there is a swing towards Culture-free tests. These are tests that use logic rather than word knowledge, so that diagrams are used instead of words. This makes no difference to the outcome, as spacial understanding and logical reasoning are good guides to one's degree of intelligence. These tests have also been standardised.

The eight tests which have been specially compiled for this book include about 40 per cent culture-free questions. The tests have not been standardised, so an IQ assessment has not been given. They are designed for practice for readers intending to take IQ tests in the future, and a guide is given as a check of success in undertaking each of these eight separate tests. There is also a further accumulated score for performance in all eight tests.

It is now considered that one's IQ factor has a hereditary basis, but that it is possible to improve slightly by practice with IQ tests, but only marginally. Generally speaking, the IQ factor remains constant throughout one's life, trailing off slightly with age.

How to use this book

The book consists of eight separate tests, each of 50 questions. The tests are of approximately the same degree of difficulty. It is suggested that you tackle each test separately and note your score, after checking your answers against those given at the end of each test. A scoring chart for each test is also shown, one mark being awarded for each correct answer.

Each further test taken should show a slight improvement in your score, since practice will improve performance as you get to know how questions are structured and what to expect. You will then be able to tackle subsequent similar questions with more confidence.

The total can then be taken for the eight tests and checked against the total scoring chart, shown below and also at the end of the book.

Each test has a time limit of 120 minutes which must not be exceeded.

Notes The answers to some of the questions have been explained. You may find these explanations useful if you are 'stuck' on certain types of question.

In questions where you are required to find a missing word, the number of dots shown is equal to the number of letters in the word that you are looking for.

Total scoring chart for the eight tests

160–199	Average
200–239	Good
240–319	Very Good
320–359	Excellent
360–400	Exceptional

Test 1

1 Four of these five pieces can be fitted together to form a square. Which is the odd piece out?

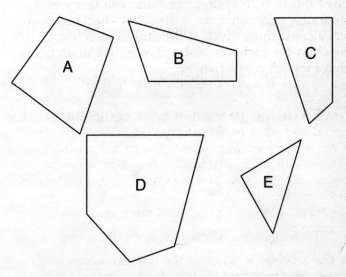

2 Complete the two 8-letter words reading clockwise. The words are synonyms.

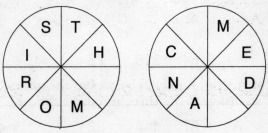

3 Which is the odd one out?

tawdry, common, gaudy, garish, brash

4   0.25, 0.25, 0.5, 1.5, ?,

Which of the numbers below comes next in the sequence above?

2.5, 3, 4.5, 5, 6

5 claim wish is an anagram of which 9-letter word?

6 Which word inside the brackets is opposite in meaning to the word in capital letters?

VESTIGIAL (vibrant, playful, complete, exterior, rudimentary)

7

Which hexagon below continues the above sequence?

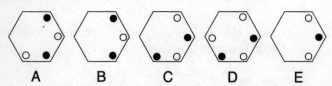

A	B	C	D	E

8   54 : 216 : 72

Which set of numbers below has the same relationship as the three numbers above?

        A   37 : 111 : 52
        B   72 : 288 : 96
        C   84 : 336 : 84
        D   78 : 296 : 98
        E   27 : 59 : 16

9 Which of these is not an anagram of a colour shade?

- (a) RE ICES
- (b) INSANE
- (c) NICE ARM
- (d) DENT PAN
- (e) SUREST

10 Insert the word in the brackets that means the same as the definitions outside the brackets.

small building (. . . .) cast off

11 42783, 3874, 478, ? ,

What comes next?

12 What creature should appear in the brackets reading downwards to complete the 3-letter words?

EA ( )
ER ( )
HO ( )
RI ( )
SK ( )
CA ( )

13 Which word inside the brackets means the same as the word in capital letters?

PAUCITY (mendicant, dearth, security, aid, cessation)

14 Single is to one as cipher is to:

a hundred, ten, five, two , zero

15 Which of the triangles A to E is missing from the top of the pyramid?

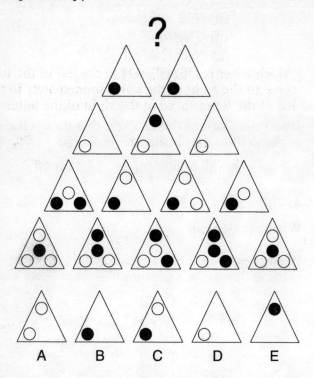

16 Place two letters in each set of brackets so that they finish the word on the left and start the word on the right. You must choose the correct letters so that when read in pairs, downwards, they will spell out an eight-letter word.

JU (. .) ME

GA (. .) LT

LA (. .) UN

EP (. .) ON

17 What number continues this sequence?

1, 1.5, 0.75, 1.75, 0.5, ? ,

18   A B C D E F G H

Which letter is immediately to the left of the letter
three to the right of the letter immediately to the
left of the letter three to the right of the letter B?

19

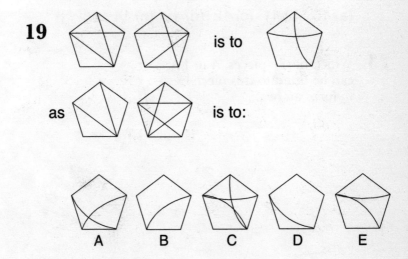

20 Use every letter of the phrase below, once only, to
spell out three types of fruit.

THE EARLY DIVORCE

21 Which word inside the brackets is opposite in
meaning to the word in capital letters?

INNATE (essential, overt, unnatural, congenital,
            unfamiliar)

22 Which of the numbers, (a) to (e), should replace the question mark?

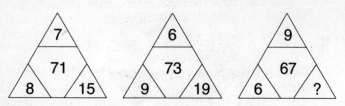

(a) 10 (b) 11 (c) 12 (d) 13 (e) 14

23 Which of the pieces, A to E, can be fitted to this piece to form an oval?

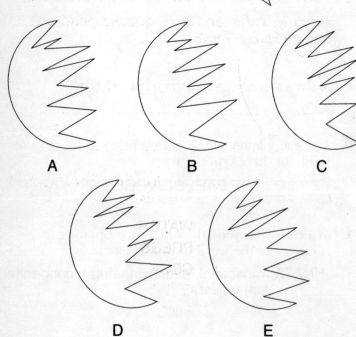

A   B   C

D   E

24 Which of these is a repast?

    (a) A rest
    (b) A witty reply
    (c) A meal
    (d) A return
    (e) An annulment

25 Which familiar phrase is represented by the diagram?

Clue: New course

(Word lengths 1, 6, 2, 9)

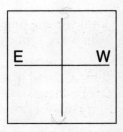

26 Which two of these words are closest in meaning?

temerity, instantaneously, gratuity, pourbois, perpendicular, treaties

27 Make a word. Clue: VERTICAL HEIGHT.

T	U	D	I	T	A	L	E

28 Find a word which when placed in front of each of these words makes new words.

                        WATCH
                        PRESS
   (_ _ _ _) COCK
                        OVER
                        PING

29 2, 8, 7, 10, 40, 39, 42, 168, 167, ? ,

What comes next in the above sequence?

30 Place a word inside the brackets which means the same as the words outside the brackets.

irritate (. . . . .) cotton fabric

31 Find the missing letters to make two 8-letter words which are synonyms. The words run clockwise.

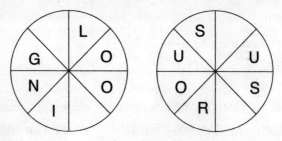

32 Which of the words below would you connect with gnomon?

plant, dwarf, sundial, ditch, cannon

33 Trace out a 10-letter word by travelling along the lines. Clue: LIMITS.

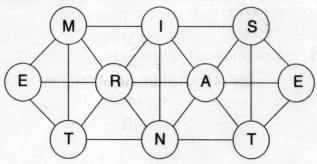

18

34 Which two words are closest in meaning?

sensationalism, poseur, quench, mediocrity, slake, panache

35 Which of the circles A–E is missing from the top of the diagram?

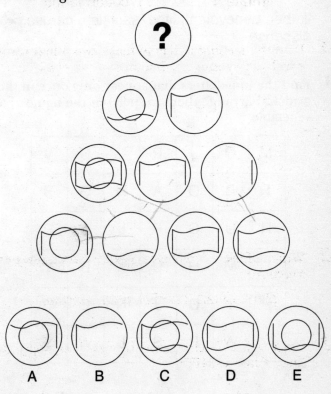

A   B   C   D   E

36 Which is the odd one out?

jowl, chin, cheek, shoulder, jaw

37 Find an amusing version of a well-known saying. The vowels have been omitted and word boundaries altered.

FTFRS TYDNT SCCDG VP

38 Which two of these words are similar in meaning?

limber, benevolent, lithe, sacrifice, peruse, dispense

39 Find the nine letters that appear only once in the grid and arrange them to spell out the name of a vegetable.

M	O	J	P	D	C	V
F	B	Q	A	N	G	S
R	U	G	F	L	T	P
L	M	H	U	K	B	Y
P	I	D	J	N	E	Q
V	W	P	S	L	W	Y

40 If meat in a river is T(HAM)ES (6 letters) and monkey in church is CH(APE)L (6 letters), can you find a composer's name in lights (10 letters)?

41 Find a one-word anagram:

O dice man

20

42 Find a word which when placed in front of each of these words makes new words.

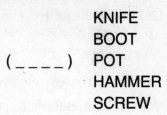

          KNIFE

          BOOT

(_ _ _ _) POT

          HAMMER

          SCREW

43 Which number should replace the question mark?

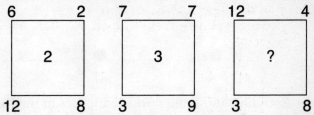

44 Place three of the 2-letter 'bits' together to make a cavity.

ba, cu, la, na, da, te

45 Which number should replace the question mark?

6	7	3	39
7	2	4	10
8	?	8	40
9	4	3	33

46 Change one letter only in each word to make a well-known phrase.

GO BAKE PLACE

47

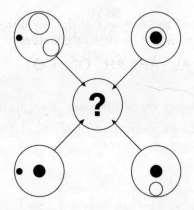

Each line and symbol which appears in the four outer circles, above, is transferred to the centre circle according to these rules:

If a line or symbol occurs in the outer circles:

once:	it is transferred
twice:	it is possibly transferred
3 times:	it is transferred
4 times:	it is not transferred

Which of the circles A, B, C, D or E, shown below should appear at the centre of the diagram above?

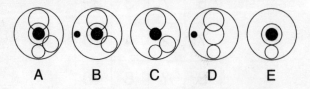

A   B   C   D   E

48 Find the answer:

$$\frac{3}{9} \div \frac{1}{8} = ?$$

49 Select four of the five sets of double letters, and rearrange to make an Australian tree.

AL, AB, AH, OL, CO

50 With the aid of the clue, insert the letters into the grid, to find the two words.

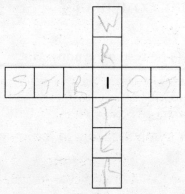

E S R P W R T T R C

Clue: literary lines person

23

Answers to Test 1

1 A.

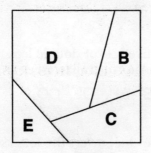

2 HUMORIST, COMEDIAN

3 common (The rest are synonyms.)

4 6. (× 1, × 2, × 3, × 4)

5 whimsical

6 complete

7 A. (The black dot moves one corner clockwise at each stage and a white, then black, dot is added to it at each stage.)

8 B 72 : 288 : 96. (72 × 4 = 288, ÷ 3 = 96)

9 (d). DENT PAN = pendant. (The colour shades are: cerise (RE ICES), sienna (INSANE), carmine (NICE ARM), russet (SUREST).)

10 shed

11 87. (Reverse the previous number each time and drop the lowest digit.)

12 RABBIT. (To give EAR, ERA, HOB, RIB, SKI, CAT.)

13 dearth

14 zero

15 D. (The contents of each triangle are determined by the contents of the two triangles immediately below it. Only when circles appear in the same position in these two triangles are they carried forward to the triangle above, and then they change from white to black and vice versa.)

16 DOMESTIC

17 2. (Add 0.5, then deduct 0.75, then add 1, then deduct 1.25 then add 1.5.)

18 F.

19 D. (Only lines which are common to the first two pentagons are carried forward to the final figure, in which they become curved lines.)

20 OLIVE, CHERRY, DATE

21 unnatural

22 (d) 13. ($9 \times 6 + 13 = 67$)

23 B.

24 (c) A meal

25 A change of direction

26 pourbois, gratuity

27 ALTITUDE

28 STOP

29 170. (The sequence goes $\times$ 4, $-$ 1, $+$ 3, and is repeated.)

30 pique

31 BLOOMING, LUSTROUS

32 sundial

33 TERMINATES

34 slake, quench

35 C. (The contents of each circle are determined by the contents of the two circles immediately below it. These are combined, but symbols which are the same disappear.)

36 shoulder. (It is below the neck, the rest are above.)

37 IF AT FIRST YOU DON'T SUCCEED GIVE UP

38 limber, lithe

39 ARTICHOKE

40 C(HANDEL)IER

41 Comedian

42 JACK

43 8. $\left(\dfrac{6 \times 8}{12 \times 2} = 2, \ \dfrac{7 \times 9}{7 \times 3} = 3, \ \dfrac{12 \times 8}{3 \times 4} = 8 \right)$

44 lacuna

45 6. (6 × 7 = 42, − 3 = 39
　　　7 × 2 = 14, − 4 = 10
　　　8 × 6 = 48, − 8 = 40
　　　9 × 4 = 36, − 3 = 33)

46 TO MAKE PEACE

47 A.

48 2⅔. $\left(\dfrac{3}{9} \div \dfrac{1}{8} = \dfrac{3}{9} \times \dfrac{8}{1} = \dfrac{24}{9} = 2\dfrac{2}{3} \right)$

49 COOLABAH

50 SCRIPT WRITER

Scoring Chart for Test 1

20–24	Average
25–29	Good
30–39	Very Good
40–44	Excellent
45–50	Exceptional

Test 2

1

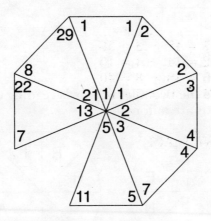

Which of A to E is the missing section?

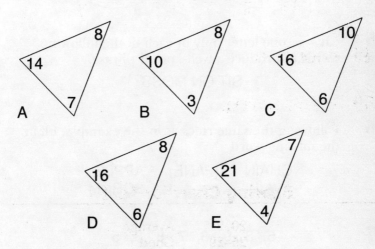

2   vice stepper is an anagram of which 11-letter word?

3

Which option comes next in the above sequence?

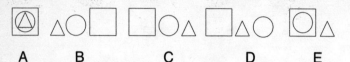

  A   B   C   D   E

4 Complete the two 8-letter words reading clockwise. The words are antonyms.

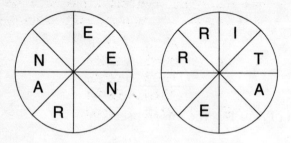

5 Change one letter only in each of the following words to produce a well-known phrase.

SIT ON MOSS

6 Following the same rules as in the example, fill in the missing word.

     CHAIN   (PANE)   APPLE
     AVAIL   (. . . .)   SCRUM

7   5, 3 , 9, 8, 7, 8, 3, 5

What is the difference between the average of these numbers and the second highest odd number?

8   Which of A, B, C, D or E is the odd one out?

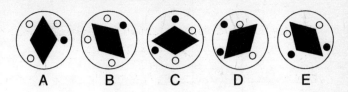

A   B   C   D   E

9
9821 : 8532
7364 : 2727

Which pair of numbers below has the same
relationship as the numbers in the examples above?

A   4912 : 2718
B   3649 : 1832
C   7699 : 6223
D   9816 : 6918
E   4212 : 3216

10 Which word means both secure and run away?

11 Which two of these words are most opposite in
meaning?

weak, specific, facile, sincere, difficult, unreal

12 What number is 56 less than when it is multiplied
by 8 times itself?

13 College is to noun as acute is to:

pronoun, adjective, verb, conjunction, adverb

14 Which of A, B, C, D or E is the missing tile?

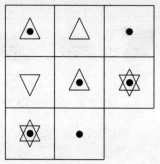

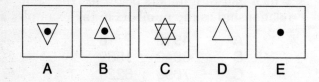

A   B   C   D   E

15 Find the starting point and move from square to square horizontally or vertically to spell out a 12-letter word. You must provide the missing letters.

N		R
I	D	O
C		N
	I	O

16 What is the missing number?

1	2	5	1	2	7
2	4	4	3	8	1
3	2	2	?	1	1
4	3	1	4	3	6

17 1372, 1384, 1399, 1420, 1426, ? ,

Which of the numbers below continues the sequence above?

1432, 1436, 1438, 1452, 1456

18 Which of A, B, C, D or E comes next in this sequence?

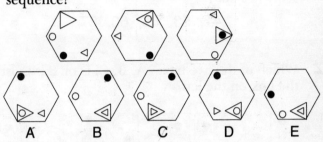

P	Y	D	Z	J	W	C	N
J	Z	O	G	N	O	R	K
I	A	R	V	L	X	T	F
S	F	J	E	Q	I	S	P
H	Q	K	W	D	V	M	L
O	X	B	N	Y	D	R	G

19

There are just seven letters that appear only once in the above grid. Which Shakespeare character can these be arranged to spell out?

20 Insert the word in the brackets that means the same as the words outside the brackets.

Greek goddess   (. . . .)   ponder

21   49, 59, 55, 53, 61, 47, ? ,

Which of the numbers below comes next in the sequence above?

41, 53, 55, 63, 67

22 Which of the five boxes A, B, C, D or E is most like the box on the left?

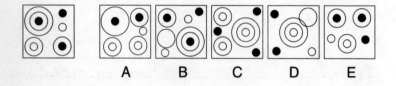

A   B   C   D   E

23 Which two of these words are closest in meaning?

animal, beseech, prey, target, weapon, help

24 A linen hat is an anagram of which boy's name?

25 Make a word.
Clue: USED FOR LIFTING.

| L | A | W | I | S | S | N | D |

26

Which of the numbers, (a) to (e), should replace the question mark?

(a) 120 (b) 125 (c) 186 (d) 266 (e) 304

27 What is the meaning of lacteal?

        (a)   elastic
        (b)   milky
        (c)   woven
        (d)   praise
        (e)   principal

28 Find the saying. The vowels have been omitted and word boundaries altered.

FLNDH SMNYR SNPRT D

29 Which is the odd one out?

carpenter, plumber, ostler, electrician, roofer, plasterer

30 Which two of these words are closest in meaning?

carousal, milieu, profound, idiocy, surroundings, attenuation

31 Which number should replace the question mark?

7, 13¼, 8½, 11, 10, 8¾, ?,

32 Find a word which, when placed in front of each of these words, makes new words.

(_ _ _ _ _)
TAKER
WRITER
VALUE
TOW
STATE

33 Trace out a 10-letter word travelling along the lines. Clue: DESTROY.

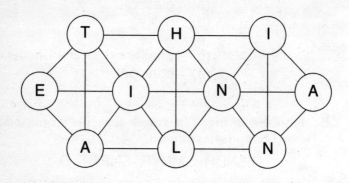

34 Place three of the 2-letter 'bits' together to make the universe.

sm, he, co, in, os, av

35 Make a 6-letter word using only these four letters.

M   S
C   I

36

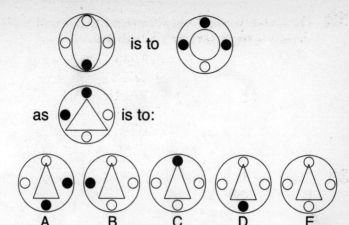

37 Which number should replace the question mark?

38 Place a word inside the brackets which means the same as the words outside the brackets.

pledge (. . . . . .) condition

39 What is the name given to a group of otters? Is it:

      (a)   a bevy
      (b)   a cloud
      (c)   a colony
      (d)   a class?

40 Is Mohican:

jodphurs, a ravine, a tepee, a hair style,
a crescent?

41 Find the missing letters to make two 8-letter words which are synonyms. The words both run clockwise.

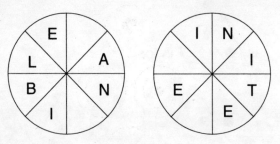

42 Fine a one-word anagram:

pares aid

43 What is a promontory? Is it:

(a)   a promenade
(b)   a headland
(c)   a cave
(d)   an island
(e)   a lagoon?

44 Find a word which, when placed in front of each of these words, makes new words.

(. . .)
LASH
LID
GLASS
WASH
SIGHT

45 Select four of the five sets of double letters and rearrange them to make a horse.

LI, AL, ST, FI, ON

46 Which of the circles A to E replaces the question mark from the top of the pyramid?

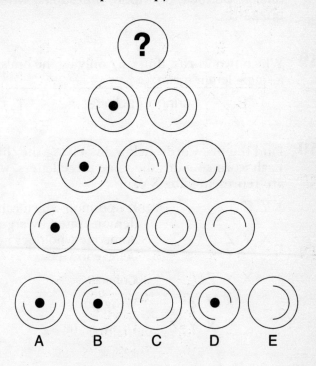

47 Which number should replace the question mark?

7	6	4	34
9	6	7	69
7	6	2	20
8	7	7	?

48 Which two of these words are similar in meaning?

niblick, puttock, crampon, marsupial, whey, buzzard

49 Which two words, differing only by the omission of a single letter, mean:

cringe / admirer

50 Find the five words, below, by solving the clues. Each word contains the same three letters, which are represented by XYZ.

X Y Z _ _ _ _   Proposition which can be demonstrated by argument.

_ X Y Z _ _ _   Someone who does not believe in God.

_ _ X Y Z _ _   Collects.

_ _ _ X Y Z _   Wing part.

_ _ _ _ X Y Z   Draw air in.

Answers Test 2

1   D. (There are three sequences running around the
     octagon all starting with the section containing
     three 1s.
     The first, in the left-hand corner of each
     section, runs 1, 2, 3, 4, 5 etc. The second, in the
     right-hand corner, runs 1, 2, 4, 7 etc. that, is
     +1, +2, +3, +4, etc. The third, in the centre,
     runs 1, 1, 2, 3, 5, 8, 13, 21. That is, each
     number is the sum of the previous two.)

2   perspective

3   C. (The triangle is moving from left to right, one
     step at a time.)

4   ENTRANCE, IRRITATE

5   HIT OR MISS

6   CALM. $\left(\underset{2\ \ 3}{AVAIL}\ \underset{1\,2\ \,34}{(CALM)}\ \underset{1\ \ \ \ \ 4}{SCRUM}\right)$

7   1.

8   D. (A and B are the same figure rotated.
        C and E are the same figure rotated.)

9 A 4912 : 2718.
(Reverse and subtract; 4912 – 2194 = 2718.)

10 bolt

11 facile, difficult

12 8.

13 adjective

14 C. (Looking both across and down, anything
common to the first two squares is not carried
forward to the third square.)

15 INTRODUCTION

16 5. (The sum of each column of numbers increases
by one each time, that is, 10, 11, 12, 13, 14, 15.)

17 1438. (Each number is made up of the previous
number plus the sum of its last three digits.
1426 + 4 + 2 + 6 = 1438.)

18 B. (The white circle moves two corners clockwise at
each stage.
The black circle moves one corner
anticlockwise at each stage.
The large triangle moves one corner clockwise
and the small triangle two corners at each stage.

43

19 MACBETH

20 muse

21 67. (There are two sequences, alternating. The first starts with 49 and adds 6 each time. The second starts with 59 and subtracts 6 each time.)

22 B. (It, also, contains one large circle, three medium sized circles, three black small circles and two white small circles.)

23 prey, target

24 Nathaniel

25 WINDLASS

26 (d) 266. $((31 - 17) \times (58 - 39))$ in the same pattern as the other two circles.

27 (b) milky

28 A FOOL AND HIS MONEY ARE SOON PARTED

29 ostler. (The rest are building tradesmen.)

30 milieu, surroundings

31 11½. (There are two series (+1½), 7, 8½, 10, 11½, and (–2¼) 13¼, 11, 8¾, 6½)

32 UNDER

33 ANNIHILATE

34 cosmos

35 MIMICS

36 A. (The oval shape is flattened to a circle, so the triangle is flattened. The small circles change from black to white and from white to black.)

37 14. $((13 - 7) + (4 + 9) = 19,$
$(14 - 8) + (8 + 8) = 22,$
$(17 - 9) + (4 + 2) = 14)$

38 plight

39 a bevy

40 a hair style

41 TANGIBLE, DEFINITE

42 paradise

43 (b) a headland

44 EYE

45 STALLION

46 B. (The contents of each circle are determined by the contents of the two circles immediately below it. These combine, but symbols which are the same disappear.)

47 63. $(7 \times 4 = 28, + 6 = 34$
$9 \times 7 = 63, + 6 = 69$
$7 \times 2 = 14, + 6 = 20$
$8 \times 7 = 56, + 7 = 63)$

48 puttock, buzzard

49 fawn/fan

50 theorem, atheist, gathers, feather, breathe.
$(XYZ = the)$

Scoring Chart for Test 2

20–24	Average
25–29	Good
30–39	Very Good
40–44	Excellent
45–50	Exceptional

Test 3

1   Complete the two words,
    one reading clockwise and
    the other reading
    anticlockwise. One goes
    round the outer circle
    and the other round the
    inner circle. The two
    words are synonyms. You
    must provide the missing
    letters.

2   Change one letter only in each of the following
    words to produce a well-known phrase:

AIM ON ARE

3

15	3	25	36
16	7	5	8
10	6	2	11
18	4	27	9

What is the difference between the square of the
lowest cube number and the cube of the lowest
square number in the above grid?

4   Which of A, B, C, D or E is the missing tile?

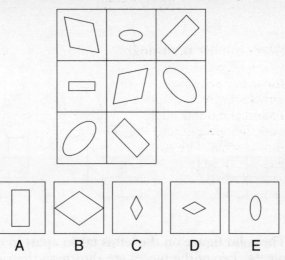

A   B   C   D   E

5   Complete the five words so that two letters are
common to each word. That is, the same two letters
that end the first word also start the second word,
and so on. The two letters that end the fifth word
are the first two letters of the first word, thus
completing the circle.

_ _ E T _ _

_ _ A V _ _

_ _ D E _ _

_ _ C A _ _

_ _ B A _ _

6   What item of clothing is suggested by the following?

7

```
36  ( 654  )  29
72  ( 5618 )  89
84  (  ?   )  22
```

What number is missing?

8

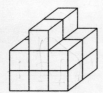

The solid figure on the left is taken apart in three pieces. Two of the pieces are shown on the right above. Which one of the options A to C is the third piece?

A   B   C

9   **THE SAD CITIES**

The above is an anagram of which well-known phrase? Clue: IRREVOCABLE DECISION.

10 What number should replace the question mark?

7	?	5
2	4	6
3	8	1

11 What 3-letter word can be placed behind each set of letters to form four new words?

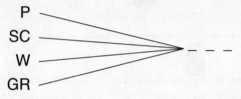

P
SC
W
GR
– – –

12 Which is the odd one out?

enhance, exacerbate, elevate, exalt

13

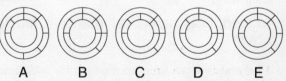

Which of A, B, C, D or E continues the above sequence?

A   B   C   D   E

14 The houses are numbered 1, 2, 3, 4 etc. up one side of the street, then back down the other side. Opposite number 23 is number 48. The houses are all identical. How many are there in the street?

15 faint icings is an anagram of which 11-letter word?

16 Which of A to E is the odd one out?

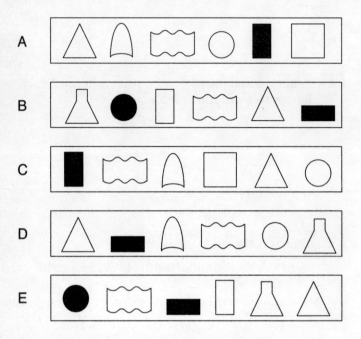

17 Which two of these words are most opposite in meaning?

rugged, diligent, critical, practical, indifferent, brave

18 How many minutes before midnight is it if one hour ago it was five times as many minutes past 9 p.m.?

19

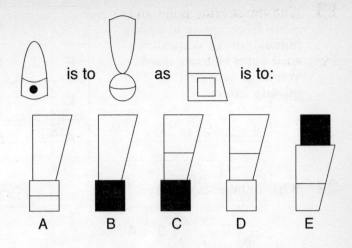

A   B   C   D   E

20 Which word inside the brackets means the same as the word in capital letters?

LEGATEE (decree, plaintiff, deed, beneficiary, garnishee)

21 The name of which country can be placed in the brackets, reading downwards, to complete the three-letter words?

BA ( )
AG ( )
JA ( )
HO ( )
SE ( )
BU ( )

22 468952 is to 926845 as
237198 is to which of these?

(a) 474396 (b) 798321 (c) 183729 (d) 584291
(e) 738912

23 Find the starting point and move from square to square horizontally or vertically to spell out a 12-letter word. You must provide the missing letters.

V	R	U
E	I	S
L	L	
A		C

24 What number is missing?

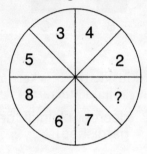

25 What is the longest word that can be made from this set of letters using each letter only once?

TARMUHIEC

26 Place three of the 2-letter 'bits' together to make a coin.

ek, do, sh, ra, da, el

27 Which number should replace the question mark in this sequence?

7⅝, 14¾, 21⅛, ? ,

28 Find a word which when placed in front of these words makes new words.

THROW
                                   BEAR
(_ _ _ _)   TAKE
                                   WROUGHT
                                   POWER

29 Make a word. Clue: UNRULY BOY.

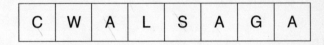

C	W	A	L	S	A	G	A

30 Which is the odd one out sequentially?

fedora, accent, tipple, foible, effect, tandem

31 Trace out a 10-letter word by travelling along the lines. Clue: DOGS.

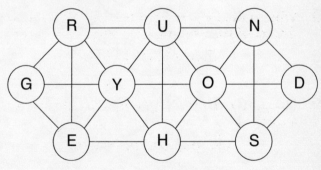

32 Place a word inside the brackets that means the same as the words outside the brackets.

steal game (. . . . .) cook

33 What is an oubliette?

(a) a dungeon
(b) a tunnel
(c) a gargoyle
(d) a sybil
(e) a spectre

34 Which two of these words are closest in meaning?

fortitude, platform, caprice, banality, perron, changeling

35 Which of the circles A to E replaces the question mark from the top of this pyramid?

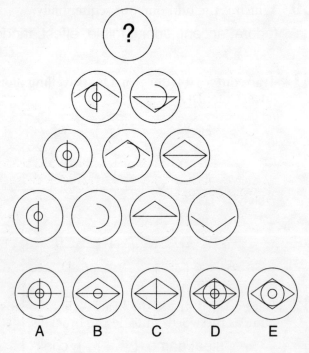

36 Find the amusing variation of a well-known saying. The vowels have been omitted and word boundaries altered.

TMNYC KSSPL THBRT HBTSC NN

37 What is a parka? Is it:

- (a) a jacket
- (b) an open space
- (c) recreation
- (d) a parking lot
- (e) a shoe?

38 Which number should replace the question mark?

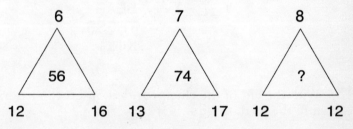

39 Find the missing letters to make two words which are synonyms. One word runs clockwise and the other anticlockwise.

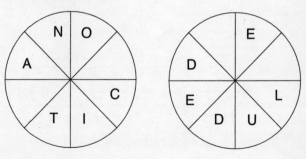

40 Which two of these words are similar in meaning?

confuse, moider, weary, parsimonious, helpless, boisterous

41 Make a 6-letter word using only these four letters.

C   I

R   T

42 Find a word which when placed in front of these words makes new words.

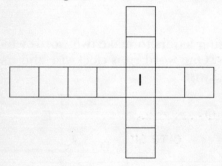

(_ _ _)

MAT
GET
BEAR
TRESS
KING

43 With the aid of the clue provided, insert the letters into the gird, to find the two words.

R G P T T U O N N N

Clue: reversal of fortune.

44 Complete the hyphenated word. Clue: congenial.

_ _ OD-HU _ _ _ _ _ _

45 Which of the circles A to E replaces the question mark?

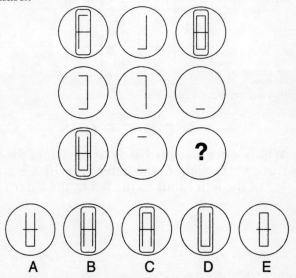

46 0, 1, −1, 0, −2, ? ,

What comes next?

47 Find a one-word anagram:

cure sir

48 Select four of the five sets of double letters and rearrange to make pure.

IS, PR, TI, NE, IN

49 Which number should replace the question mark?

80	8	7	17
72	9	8	16
64	8	10	18
72	8	11	?

50   A B C D E F G H

Which letter is immediately to the left of the letter three to the right of the letter immediately to the left of the letter four to the left of the letter G?

Answers Test 3

1 SCARCITY, SHORTAGE

2 ARM IN ARM

3 0. $(8 \times 8 = 64,\quad 8 = \text{lowest cube}$
$4 \times 4 \times 4 = 64,\quad 4 = \text{lowest square})$

4 D. (In the array there are three diamonds, three ellipses and three rectangles. Each line down and across contains one of these three figures reduced in size and lying horizontal.)

5 TEETHE, HEAVEN, ENDEAR, ARCADE, DEBATE

6 headsquare

7 168. $(3 \times 2 = 6,\ 6 \times 9 = 54;\ 7 \times 8 = 56,$
$2 \times 9 = 18;\ 8 \times 2 = 16, 4 \times 2 = 8)$

8 B.

9 THE DIE IS CAST

10 0. (So each horizontal, vertical and corner-to-corner line totals 12.)

11 ANT

12 exacerbate (It means to increase the problem. The others mean to increase the power.)

13 E. (In each ring another line is added at each stage, moving clockwise.)

14 70. (Opposite house numbers add up to 71. So 1 is opposite the last number, 70.)

15 significant

16 D. (A contains the same symbols as C. B contains the same symbols as E.)

17 diligent, indifferent

18 20 minutes

19 B. (The square enlarges and changes from white to black. The quadrilateral inverts and goes on top of the square. The line goes in the square but is not visible as both are black.)

20 beneficiary

21 NORWAY (To give BAN, AGO, JAR, HOW, SEA, BUY.)

22 (c) 183729. (2 3 7 1 9 8
             1 8 3 7 2 9)

23 SURVEILLANCE

24 5. (Opposite numbers total 10.)

25 RHEUMATIC

26 shekel

27 $27\tfrac{7}{8}$. ($+\ 6\tfrac{3}{4}$ each time.)

28 OVER

29 SCALAWAG

30 foible. (Each word commences with the last letter
                of the previous word except for foible.)

31 GREYHOUNDS

32 poach

33 (a) a dungeon

34 perron, platform

35 D. (The contents of each circle are determined by the contents of the two circles immediately below it. These combine, but symbols which are the same disappear.)

36 TOO MANY COOKS SPOIL THE BROTH BUT SO CAN ONE

37 (a) a jacket

38 84. $((6 \times 12) - 16 = 56, (7 \times 13) - 17 = 74, (8 \times 12) - 12 = 84)$

39 MONASTIC, SECLUDED

40 moider, confuse

41 CRITIC

42 FOR

43 TURNING POINT

44 GOOD-HUMOURED

45 C. (Looking both across and down, anything common to the first two squares is not carried forward to the third square.)

46 –1. (The sequence goes +1, –2, +1, –2, +1, etc.)

47 cruiser

48 PRISTINE

49 20. (80 ÷ 8 = 10, + 7 = 17
72 ÷ 9 = 8, + 8 = 16
64 ÷ 8 = 8, + 10 = 18
72 ÷ 8 = 9, + 11 = 20)

50 D.

Scoring Chart for Test 3

20–24	Average
25–29	Good
30–39	Very Good
40–44	Excellent
45–50	Exceptional

Test 4

1

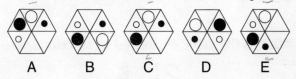

Which of A to E continues the above sequence?

A B C D E

2 Which of the numbers, (a) to (e), comes next in this sequence?

2, 2, 4, 12, 48, 48, 96, ? ,

(a) 192 (b) 208 (c) 288 (d) 304 (e) 344

3 Which of A to E is the odd one out?

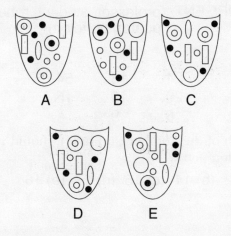

A B C

D E

4 Which of the words, (a) to (e), is missing from the brackets?

BEND   (LOOPHOLE)   LAIR

HALT   (. . . . .)   LEAF

(a) SNUGNESS (b) STUDFARM
(c) TIMEBOMB (d) LIVEWIRE
(e) STOPPAGE

5 What is the value expressed as a decimal of:

$$2\tfrac{1}{2} \div \tfrac{5}{7}$$

6 What phrase is represented by the diagram?
Clue: Change course.

LADEP

7 Which word inside the brackets means the same as the word in capital letters?

INSURGENT (professor, student, rebel,
                    guarantor, felon)

8

24	18	54
20	10	15
6	9	?

Which of the numbers, (a) to (e), should replace the question mark?

(a) 12 (b) 14 (c) 16 (d) 17 (e) 18

9 Complete the two 8-letter words, one reading clockwise and the other reading anticlockwise. One is found round the outer circle and the other round the inner circle. The two words are antonyms. You must provide the missing letters.

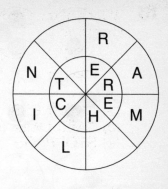

10 Which of these is not an anagram of a Greek or Roman god/goddess?

    (a)   CURRY ME
    (b)   HAIR TOO
    (c)   PEN TUNE
    (d)   SPOON DIE
    (e)   ADOPT HEIR

11 Insert the word in the brackets that means the same as the definitions outside the brackets.

incandescence   (. . . . .)   underweight

12

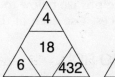

Which of the numbers, (a) to (e), should replace the question mark?

(a) 21 (b) 22 (c) 23 (d) 24 (e) 25

13

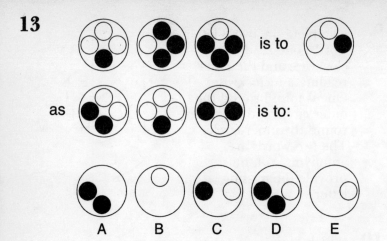

14 Complete the words with the aid of the clues. The same three letters appear in each word and these letters are represented by the letters XYZ.

X Y Z _ _ _ _ Type of machine found in arcades

_ X Y Z _ _ _ Point of view

_ _ X Y Z _ _ Encroach

_ _ _ X Y Z _ Assisting

_ _ _ _ X Y Z Chief thing or person

15 Arrange all the letters of the phrase below to spell out the names of three dances. Use each of the letters once only.

KEEP BARE LOO ROLL

16 Which 3-digit number continues this sequence?

276, 395, 427, 639, ? ,

17 Which of these is the odd one out?

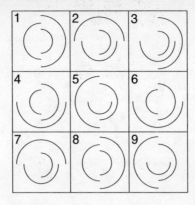

18 Which Biblical figure can be placed in the brackets reading downwards to complete the 3-letter words?

HA ( )
LE ( )
RA ( )
HI ( )
TO ( )
FI ( )

19   19 : 132 : 923

Which set of numbers below has the same relationship as the three numbers above?

A   25 : 174 : 1217
B   18 :   34 :   66
C   23 : 161 : 1127
D   12 :   73 :   433
E   2 :   18 :   54

71

20 Which of the pentagons A to E is the missing one?

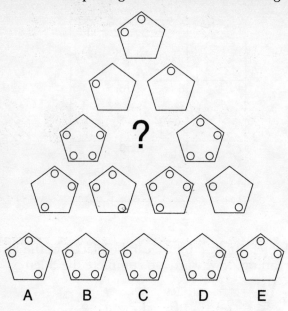

A B C D E

21 Change BOOK to MARK with four links by changing one letter at a time at each stage, each link making a proper word.

BOOK

· · · ·

· · · ·

· · · ·

MARK

22 Change one letter from each of the following words to produce a well-known phrase:

SO TO DO PEA

23

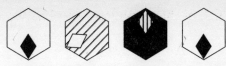

Which of A, B, C, D or E continues the above sequence?

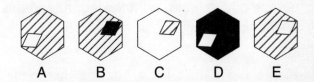

24 Which two of the following words have opposite meanings?

chatter, garble, amass, decipher, undress, understand

25 Which word is the odd one out?

borrow, nodded, Nelson, Norway, nadir, sapid

26 Make a word. Clue: RUBBISH.

P	U	R	T	Y	M	E	R

27 Find a word which when placed in front of each of these words makes new words.

$$(\_ \_ \_ \_)$$

SOME
GRIP
BAG
HOLD
PICKED

28 Find the answer as a whole number and a fraction.

$$6\tfrac{7}{8} + 4\tfrac{3}{5} - 2\tfrac{1}{10}$$

29 Which two of these words are closest in meaning?

serendipity, retinue, genuflexing, attendants, spiritual, cardinal

30 Place three of the 2-letter 'bits' together to make strictness.

re, ga, ri, ra, go, ur

31 Trace out a 10-letter word by travelling along the lines. Clue: MONSTER.

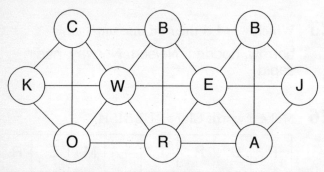

32 Place a word inside the brackets which means the same as the words outside the brackets.

decline (. . . . . .) rubbish

33 What is a pavlova? Is it:

(a) a dance (b) a star (c) a dessert
(d) a penance (e) a chapel?

34 Which two of these words are similar in meaning?

ageing, soliloquy, transmit, senescent, remembrance, derivative

35 Find the saying. The vowels have been omitted and word boundaries altered.

THQCK STWYT MNSHR TSTHR GHHSS TMCH

36 Which of the circles A to E replaces the question mark from the top of the pyramid?

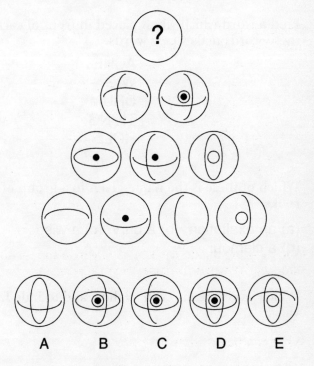

37 At a recent village council election for mayor, a total of 963 votes were cast for the four candidates, the winner exceeding his opponents by 55, 79 and 103 votes respectively. How many votes were cast for each candidate?

38 Which number should replace the question mark?

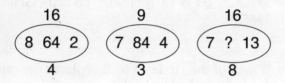

39 Find a word which when placed in front of each of these words makes new words.

ACHE
WIG
(. . .)   DRUM
THING
HOLE

40 Which of these is the name given to a group of rooks?

(a) an exaltation (b) a bury (c) a wisp
(d) a clamour

41 Which word means both to show and to hide from view?

42 Which number should replace the question mark?

49	7	8	15
64	8	9	17
26	2	13	26
20	5	9	?

43 What is a quintal? Is it:

(a) a diatribe (b) a fish (c) a desert
(d) a weight (e) a thong?

44 Find a one-word anagram:

le mon ode

45 Select four of the five sets of double letters and rearrange to make a worm.

TO, DO, DE, MA, NE

46 What is ferine? Is it:

(a)   a salad
(b)   a wine
(c)   a moustache
(d)   a chancel
(e)   savage?

47 Each of the nine squares in the grid marked 1A to 3C, should incorporate all the lines and symbols which are shown in the squares of the same letter and number immediately above and to the left. For example, 2B should incorporate all the lines and symbols that are in 2 and B.

One of the squares is incorrect. Which one is it?

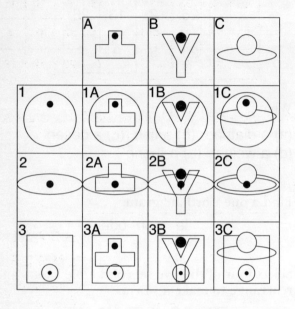

48 Find the missing letters to make two words which are synonyms. The words run clockwise.

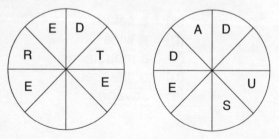

78

49 Multiply the second highest even number in the left-hand grid by the second lowest odd number in the right-hand grid.

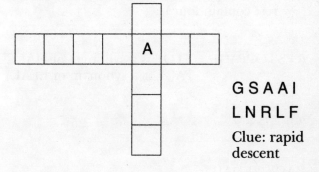

30	27	47	54
45	42	36	51
26	35	34	32
18	38	63	40

17	25	2	13
16	5	10	15
11	14	9	4
8	22	12	19

50 With the aid of the clue provided, insert the letters into the grid, to find the two words.

G S A A I
L N R L F
Clue: rapid descent

79

Answers Test 4

1   C. (The small black dot moves one segment at a time clockwise and the small white dot two segments anticlockwise.
The large black dot alternates between two segments. The large white dot moves clockwise two segments at a time.)

2   (c) 288. (The sequence goes ×1, ×2, ×3, ×4, ×1, ×2, ×3, ×4, and so on).

3   D. (It contains only three small white circles. The rest contain four.)

4   (e) STOPPAGE. (STOP is a synonym of HALT. PAGE is a synonym of LEAF.)

5   3.5. ($\frac{5}{2} \div \frac{5}{7} = \frac{5}{2} \times \frac{7}{5} = \frac{35}{10} = \frac{7}{2} = 3.5$)

6   BACK PEDAL

7   rebel

8   (e) 18. (24 ÷ 6, × 5 = 20, 18 ÷ 9, × 5 = 10, 54 ÷ 18, × 5 = 15)

9   RAMBLING, COHERENT

10 (b) HAIR TOO = Horatio.
(CURRY ME = Mercury;
PEN TUNE = Neptune;
SPOON DIE = Poseidon;
ADOPT HEIR = Aphrodite.)

11 light

12 (e) 25. $(432 \div 6 \div 4 = 18$
$612 \div 4 \div 9 = 17$
$350 \div 7 \div 2 = 25)$

13 D. (When the same circle appears in only two of
the three circles in the same position it is
transferred to the final circle. Otherwise it is
not transferred.)

14 XYZ = PIN. (pinball, opinion, impinge, helping,
kingpin.)

15 REEL, POLKA, BOLERO

16 542. (The numbers 2763954 are being repeated in
the same order.)

17 3. (All the others have an identical pairing.)

18 SAMSON (To give HAS, LEA, RAM, HIS, TOO,
FIN.)

19 A   25 : 174 : 1217. ((19 × 7) – 1 = 132,
                     (132 × 7) – 1 = 923;

                     (25 × 7) – 1 = 174,
                     (174 × 7) – 1 = 1217.)

20 D. (The contents of each pentagon are determined
        by the two pentagons below it. When a circle
        appears in the same position in the two
        pentagons below it is not carried forward to the
        pentagon above.)

21 BOOK   (This is one example.
        BOON   Readers finding other
        BORN   routes in four links are
        BARN   equally correct.)
        BARK
        MARK

22 TO GO TO SEA

23 E. (The diamond moves clockwise, first by one
        corner, then two, then three, etc.
        The hexagon alternates: white/shaded/black.
        The diamond alternates: black/white, shaded.)

24 garble, decipher

25 sapid. (The others start with a boy's name, the first
                three letters reversed.)

26 TRUMPERY

27 HAND

28 $9\frac{3}{8}$. $(6\frac{7}{8} + 4\frac{3}{5} - 2\frac{1}{10} = (6 + 4 - 2) + (\frac{35 + 24 - 4}{40})$
$= 8 + \frac{55}{40} = 9\frac{15}{40} = 9\frac{3}{8}.$

29 retinue, attendants

30 rigour

31 JABBERWOCK

32 refuse

33 (c) a dessert

34 ageing, senescent

35 THE QUICKEST WAY TO A MAN'S HEART IS THROUGH HIS STOMACH

36 D. (The contents of each circle are determined by the contents of the two circles immediately below it. These combine, but symbols which are the same disappear.)

37 300, 245, 221, 197.

(963 + 55 + 79 + 103 = 1200. Divide by 4 = 300, which is the number of winner's votes. The second candidate received 300 – 55 = 245 votes; the third received 300 – 79 = 221 votes; the fourth received 300 – 103 = 197 votes.)

38 182. ($\frac{16}{4} \times 8 \times 2 = 64$, $\frac{6}{2} \times 7 \times 4 = 84$,
$\frac{16}{8} \times 7 \times 13 = 182$)

39 EAR

40 (d) a clamour

41 screen

42 13. ($49 \div 7 = 7$, $+ 8 = 15$
$64 \div 8 = 8$, $+ 9 = 17$
$26 \div 2 = 13$, $+ 13 = 26$
$20 \div 5 = 4$, $+ 9 = 13$)

43 (d) a weight

44 melodeon

45 NEMATODE

46 (e) savage

47 2A.

48 TEMPERED, ADJUSTED

49 378. (42 × 9)

50 NIAGARA FALLS

Scoring Chart for Test 4

20–24	Average
25–29	Good
30–39	Very Good
40–44	Excellent
45–50	Exceptional

Test 5

1 To which of the boxes, A, B, C, D or E, can a dot be added so that it meets the same conditions as the box on the left?

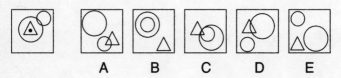

A   B   C   D   E

2 Change one letter in each of the following words to produce a well-known phrase.

ALTER ALE

3

8	12		72
4	16	?	116

Which of A to E is missing?

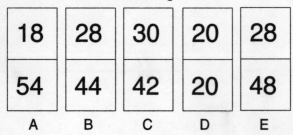

18	28	30	20	28
54	44	42	20	48
A	B	C	D	E

4   Complete the 8-letter words reading clockwise. The words are synonyms.

5   Complete the five words so that two letters are common to each word. That is, the same two letters that end the first word also start the second word, and so on. The two letters that end the fifth word are the first two letters of the first word, thus completing the circle.

```
_ _ A N _ _
_ _ L L _ _
_ _ C A _ _
_ _ B U _ _
_ _ T E _ _
```

6   Complete the two 8-letter words, one reading clockwise and the other reading anticlockwise. One is found round the outer circle and the other round the inner circle. The two words are antonyms. You must provide the missing letters.

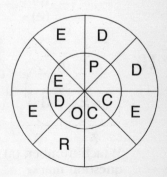

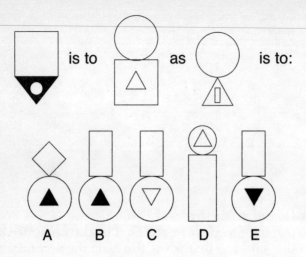

8 Which word below goes with red, king and tan?

let, row, cat, mat, pat

9 Which of these is not an anagram of an element?

(a) EDGY HORN
(b) RING NOTE
(c) THEN PEAL
(d) RICH NOEL
(e) AIM SPOUTS

10

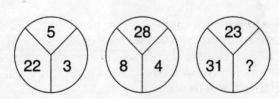

Which number, (a) to (e), should replace the
question mark?

(a) 2 (b) 3 (c) 4 (d) 5 (e) 6

11

Which of A, B, C, D or E continues this sequence?

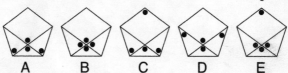

12 What phrase is represented here?

INTO A SUIT

Clue: Perplexing circumstance.

13 Which word means the same as the definitions at either side of the brackets?

repulse (. . . .) thin sheet metal

14 What is the meaning of perspicacious? Is it:

(a) lucid (b) determined (c) shrewd
(d) relevant (e) harmful?

15 Place two letters in each set of brackets so that they finish the word on the left and start the word on the right. You must choose the correct letters so that when read in pairs, downwards, they will spell out an eight-letter word.

RO (. .) AN
HE (. .) ID
FL (. .) LE
PA (. .) SS

16

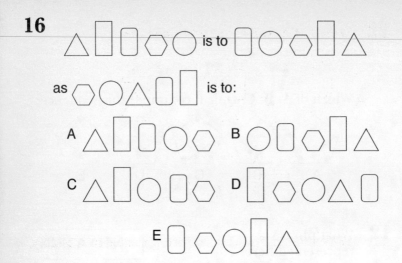

A

B

C

D

E

17 Iodine guns is an anagram of which 10-letter word?

18   A B C D E F G H

Which letter is three to the left of the letter two to the right of the letter immediately to the left of the letter F?

19 Respected is to venerable as mature is to:

healthy, vintage, old, archaic, erstwhile

20 Cyclical rioter plot is an anagram of which phrase (11, 7)? Clue: This shouldn't cause offence.

21 Join the three-letter words below to form two nine-letter words.

son, per, par, new, age, spa

22 Which of A to E is the odd one out?

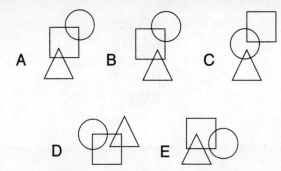

23 Which two of these words are opposite in meaning?

race, nativity, expiration, countryside, maternal, irregular

24 The name of which composer can be placed in the brackets reading downwards to complete the 3-letter words?

```
FE  (   )
SE  (   )
DI  (   )
HE  (   )
CU  (   )
FU  (   )
```

25 Which is the odd one out?

glacier, kayak, igloo, floe, frappé

26 Which word can be formed from this?

_ _ C K J _ _

27 Find a word which, when placed in front of these words, makes new words.

TRODDEN
CAST
(_ _ _ _) SIZING
PIPE
FALL

28 Trace a 10-letter word by travelling along the lines.

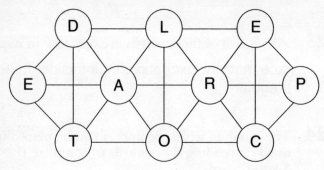

29 Which two of these words are similar in meaning?

somnambulent, recreant, precarious, reticent, cowardly, principal

30 Make a word. Clue: SHAME.

G	O	M	I	N	Y	I	N

31 Which number should replace the question mark?

6, 12, 7¼, 11¼, 8½, 10½, 9¾, 9¾, ? ,

32 Which two of these words are similar in meaning?

antecedent, anomaly, appeasement, incongruity, annotation, prestige

33 Place a word inside the brackets which means the same as the words outside the brackets.

willow (. . . . . .) sickly yellowish

34 If the score on 15 dice totals 45, what is the average of the score on the opposite sides?

35 Which of A to G is the odd one out?

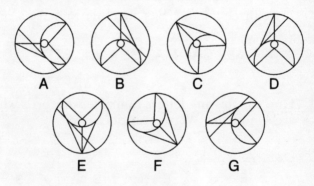

36 BATTER, ARRIVE, TRIPOD, TIPPLE, EVOLVE, ? .

Which of these words completes the above sequence? Choose from:

REDEEM, ESTATE, AVERSE, TENSER, REFERS

37 Start at one of the corner squares and move from square to square horizontally and vertically to spell out a 9-letter word. You must provide the missing letters.

	T	R
A	E	I
C		D

38 Which number should replace the question mark?

39 Place three 2-letter 'bits' together to make a small book.

AL, CA, MA, SE, NU, BO

40 Find the missing letters to make two words which are synonyms. Words run clockwise.

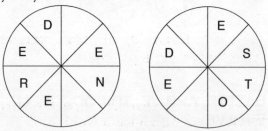

41 Which word in the brackets is opposite in meaning to the word in capital letters?

OVERWROUGHT (contrived, collected, modest, weary, tense)

94

42

2783 : 91511

Which two numbers below have the same relationship to each other as the numbers above?

A   2945 : 93762

B   1481 : 6277

C   5631 : 11944

D   4281 : 6109

E   1238 : 3512

43 With the aid of the clue, insert the letters into the grid to find the two words.

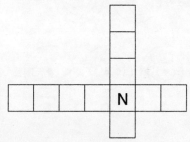

YOLSE

RETBA

Clue: gives eloquence

44 What is a talbot? Is it:

(a) a wine glass (b) a whaler (c) a car
(d) a hound (e) a picture?

45 Select four of the five sets of double letters and rearrange into an 8-letter word.

TE, TI, TO, TI, VA

46 Find a one-word anagram:

rib raze

47 Which of the circles A–E is missing from the top of the diagram?

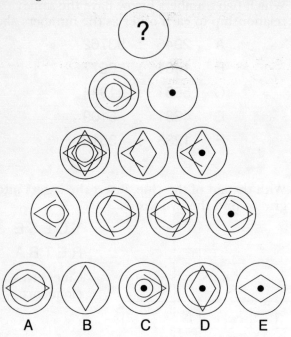

A   B   C   D   E

48 Which number should replace the question mark?

9	3	8	69
11	4	7	73
8	8	6	40
11	4	6	?

49 Find two words that have the same sound but different spellings and mean:

rapscallion / part of a church

50 Find a word which, when placed in front of these words, makes new words.

(_ _ _)

DON
BUCKLE
TAKE
ABLE
SON

Answers Test 5

1   D.   (So the dot appears in the triangle and large circle only.)

2   AFTER ALL

3   B. $\boxed{\begin{array}{c} 28 \\ \hline 44 \end{array}}$ (8 + 4 = 12, 4 + 12 = 16, 12 + 16 = 28, 16 + 28 = 44, etc.)

4   ENCUMBER, HANDICAP

5   STANCE, CELLAR, ARCANE, NEBULA, LATEST

6   DESERTED, OCCUPIED

7   E.   (The triangle turns upside-down, reduces in size, turns white to black and goes in the circle. The rectangle increases in size and goes on top of the circle.
This all corresponds to the changes in the example.)

8   row.   (All words can be prefixed by spar to form another word: sparred, sparking, spartan, sparrow.

9 (c). THEN PEAL = elephant.
(EDGY HORN = hydrogen;
RING NOTE = nitrogen;
RICH NOEL = chlorine;
AIM SPOUTS = potassium.)

10 (e) 6. $((5 + 22) \div 9 = 3; (28 + 8) \div 9 = 4;$
$(23 + 31) \div 9 = 6)$

11 B. (The dot in the left-hand segment alternates
between two corners as does the dot in the
right-hand segment.
The dot in the bottom segment moves to each
corner in turn clockwise as does the dot in the
top segment.)

12 CONFUSED SITUATION. (INTO A SUIT is an
anagram of SITUATION.)

13 foil

14 (c) shrewd

15 BEARABLE

16 A. (The figures move their positions exactly as in
the example. That is, the first figure moves
from first to last, and so on.)

17 INDIGENOUS

18 D.

19 vintage

20 POLITICALLY CORRECT

21 parsonage, newspaper

22 C. (The only one in which the circle and triangle
overlap, and not the square and triangle.)

23 NATIVITY, EXPIRATION

24 WAGNER. (FEW, SEA, DIG, HEN, CUE, FUR)

25 kayak. (The rest are made from ice.)

26 LOCKJAW

27 DOWN

28 PERCOLATED

29 recreant, cowardly

30 IGNOMINY

31 11. (There are two sequences:
(+1¼): 6, 7¼, 8½, 9¾, 11
and (–¾): 12, 11¼, 10½, 9¾, 9.)

32 anomaly, incongruity

33 sallow

34 4. (Opposite sides on a die always total 7.
On the 15 dice, therefore, opposite faces total
15 × 7 = 105. The totals on one side are 45,
so on the opposite side 105 – 45 = 60.
Average = 60 ÷ 15 = 4.)

35 E. (A is the same as D but rotated. B is the same as
G but rotated. C is the same as F but rotated.)

36 REDEEM.
(To complete a magic
word square.)

B	A	T	T	E	R
A	R	R	I	V	E
T	R	I	P	O	D
T	I	P	P	L	E
E	V	O	L	V	E
R	E	D	E	E	M

37 CARTRIDGE

38 2. $\left(\dfrac{7\times2\times6\times4}{8\times2\times3\times1} = 7, \ \dfrac{8\times4\times6\times1}{2\times4\times2\times2} = 6, \ \dfrac{10\times5\times6\times1}{5\times3\times5\times2} = 2 \right)$

39 MANUAL

40 RENDERED, BESTOWED

41 collected

42 D 4281 : 6109. (4 + 2 = 6, 2 + 8 = 10, 8 + 1 = 9.)

43 BLARNEY STONE

44 (d) a hound

45 TITIVATE

46 bizarre

47 C. (The contents of each circle are determined by
the contents of the two circles immediately
below it. These are combined, but symbols
which are the same disappear.)

48 62. (9 × 8 = 72, – 3 = 69
11 × 7 = 77, – 4 = 73
8 × 6 = 48, – 8 = 40
11 × 6 = 66, – 4 = 62)

49 knave / nave

Scoring Chart for Test 5

20–24	Average
25–29	Good
30–39	Very Good
40–44	Excellent
45–50	Exceptional

Test 6

1   Which three of the five pieces below can be fitted together to draw a cube? Choose from the options A-E.

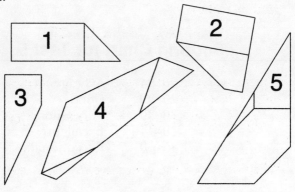

A 1, 2, 3   B 2, 4, 5   C 1, 4, 5   D 3, 4, 5
E 1, 2, 5

2   Complete the 8-letter words reading clockwise. The words are antonyms.

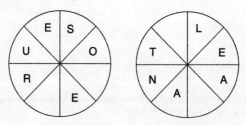

3   Indelible is to permanent as indefinite is to:

determinate, equivocal, identical, erroneous, profligate

104

4 ENEMY ALERT is an anagram of which 10-letter word?

5 5, 15, 17, 51, 53, 159, ? ,

Which of the numbers below comes next in the sequence above?

104, 126, 161, 212, 387

6 Which two nine-letter words can be formed from the six 'bits' below?

RID, DID, CAN, DEN, ATE, BED

7 Which two of these words are closest in meaning?

recent, latent, pleasing, lurking, manifest, flanking

8 Which of these is the odd one out?

dors-, fore-, noto-, retro-, ana-

9

53	(3)	59
71	(9)	79
29	(?)	98

What number should replace the question mark? Choose from:

2, 3, 4, 5, 6

10 Change one letter in each of the following words to produce a well-known phrase.

NOW I COPE

11

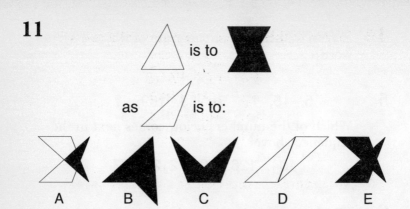

12 Which of A, B, C, D or E is the missing square?

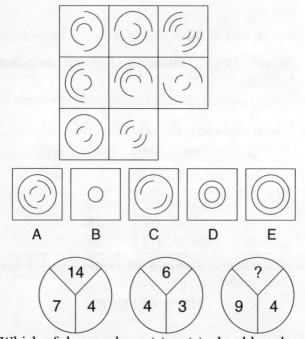

13

Which of the numbers, (a) to (e), should replace the question mark?

(a) 17 (b) 18 (c) 19 (d) 20 (e) 21

14 Which of these is not an anagram of a colour?

      (a)   EARN TIP
      (b)   FOR FANS
      (c)   CAP TRIO
      (d)   MICRONS
      (e)   LET CARS

15 What phrase is represented by the following?

16 What word can be placed in front of the following to make new words?

(a) get (b) wife (c) night (d) stream

17   357 : 466 : 575

Which three numbers below have the same relationship to one another as the three numbers above?

    A   719 : 628 : 537
    B   462 : 353 : 262
    C   246 : 462 : 624
    D   634 : 743 : 852
    E   873 : 651 : 762

18 Underline the two words that are the most opposite in meaning.

reckon, relish, contact, feed, dislike, argue

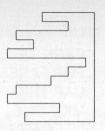

19

Which of A to D, when fitted to the above, will form a perfect square?

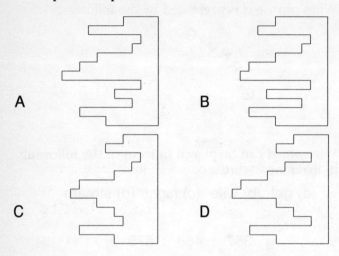

A   B

C   D

20 Which of the options A-E comes next in this sequence?

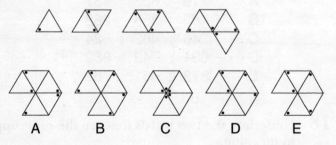

A   B   C   D   E

21 Place two letters in each set of brackets so that they finish the word on the left and start the word on the right. You must choose the correct letters so that when read in pairs, downwards, they will spell out an eight-letter word.

RI (. .) ST
HI (. .) ER
FA (. .) IR
CO (. .) AS

22

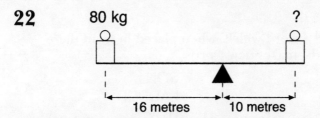

Which of these weights is required to balance the scales?

A 90 kg   B 112 kg   C 128 kg   D 130 kg
E 160 kg

23

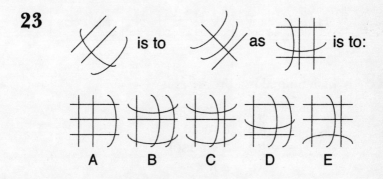

24   4 7 8 5 3 1 9 7 8 4 4 4 7 8 9 2

Multiply by five the number of even numbers which are immediately followed by an odd number in the list above. Which of these gives the result?

(a) 10   (b) 15   (c) 20   (d) 25   (e) 30

25   Use every letter of the phrase below, once only, to spell out three drinks.

BATTY PARDONER

26   Find a word which, when placed in front these words, makes new words.

(_ _ _ _)
SON
LADDER
DOWN
CHILD
FATHER

27   Make a word. Clue: PASSIONATE.

H	E	T	V	E	N	M	E

28   Which animal is a brock? Is it:

(a)   a badger
(b)   a mole
(c)   a weasel
(d)   a fox
(e)   a squirrel?

29 With the aid of the clue, insert the letters into the grid, to find the words.

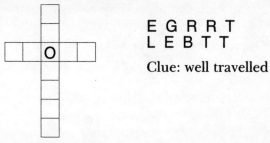

E G R R T
L E B T T

Clue: well travelled

30 Following the same rule as in the example, fill in the missing word.

DYNAMIC   (ADORN)   PROFUSE
RETORTS   (. . . . .)   LIBERTY

31 Which is the odd one out?

sabot, brogue, mitre, mule, pump

32 Place three 2-letter 'bits' together to make a crush.

UA, PR, ES, SQ, SH, ST

33 What is a teg? Is it:

(a) a knob (b) a disturbance (c) a cart
(d) a shovel (e) a sheep?

34 Place a word inside the brackets which means the same as the words outside the brackets.

graduation (. . . . .) thin plate

35

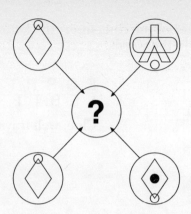

Each line and symbol which appears in the four outer circles, above, is transferred to the centre circle according to these rules:

If a line or symbol occurs in the outer circles:
once:	it is transferred
twice:	it is possibly transferred
3 times:	it is transferred
4 times:	it is not transferred

Which of the circles A, B, C, D or E, shown below should appear at the centre of the diagram, above?

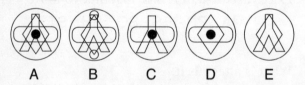

A   B   C   D   E

36 Which two of these words are similar in meaning?

stomach, maw, pancreas, gratuity, quiescent, banal

37 Find the missing letters to make two 8-letter words which are synonyms. The words run clockwise.

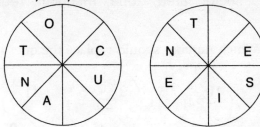

38 Find the amusing variation of a well-known saying. All of the vowels have been omitted and word boundaries altered.

HLFLF SBTTR THNNN BTWHL LFSVN BTTR

39 Find a word which, when placed in front of these words, makes new words.

(_ _ _)

PICK
CREAM
MAIDEN
SCULPTURE
BOX

40 The white dot moves two corners clockwise at each stage and the black dot moves three corners anticlockwise at each stage. In how many stages will they be together in the same corner?

41 This is an anagram of which girl's name?

AGREE BILL

42 Which of these is the odd one out?

sector, area, zone, meridian, region

43 Which number should replace the question mark?

44 What is a warrigal? Is it:

(a) a boat (b) a dingo (c) a song (d) a plaster
(e) an island?

45 Which of the circles, A to E, replaces the question mark?

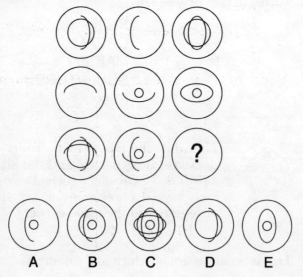

46 TOWN, OWNERS, NEBRASKA, RAILROADED,   ?

Which of these words comes next?

RAMIFICATION, ROADWORTHY, ADDITIONALLY, ROMANTICALLY, ADJUSTMENT

47 Find the answer, as a whole number and a fraction.

$$\tfrac{7}{8} \times \tfrac{3}{4} \div \tfrac{1}{8} = ?$$

48 Find a one-word anagram.

CANE GLEE

49 Select four of these three-letter words and join them to form two six-letter words that have similar meanings.

put, art, imp, ace, tor, end, rid, men

50 Which number should replace the question mark?

12	5	5	35
18	11	6	132
21	13	17	52
19	4	4	?

1   C 1, 4, 5.

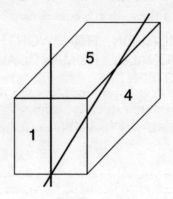

2   GRUESOME, PLEASANT

3   equivocal

4   ELEMENTARY

5   161.
(The sequence runs: × 3, + 2, × 3, + 2)

6   CANDIDATE, BEDRIDDEN

7   latent, lurking

8   fore-.
(It means in front, the rest mean back.)

9   4. ($5 \times 3 = 15$, $5 \times 9 = 45$, $45 \div 15 = 3$;
            $7 \times 1 = 7$, $7 \times 9 = 63$, $63 \div 7 = 9$;
            $2 \times 9 = 18$, $9 \times 8 = 72$, $72 \div 18 = 4$)

10 NOT A HOPE

11 E. (The original figure is turned through 180° and placed on top of the original. The resultant figure is then filled in.)

12 C. (Looking both across and down, any lines common to the first two squares are not carried forward to the third square.)

13 (b) 18. ($9 \times 4 \div 2 = 18$)

14 (a) EARN TIP = painter

       (saffron = FOR FANS, apricot = CAP TRIO, crimson = MICRONS, scarlet = LET CARS)

15 learning curve

16 mid

17 D. 634 : 743 : 852.
       (The first and second digits increase by one each time; the last digit decreases by one each time.)

18 relish, dislike

19 A.

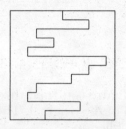

20 D. (A hexagon is being constructed by the addition of a triangle at each stage. The dots in the upward pointing triangles move anticlockwise at each stage. The dots in the downward pointing triangles move clockwise.)

21 PEDESTAL

22 C 128 kg. $((80 \times 16) \div 10 = 128)$

23 B. (All straight lines become curved, and all curved lines become straight.)

24 (c) 20.

25 PORT, TEA, BRANDY

26 STEP

27 VEHEMENT

28 (a) a badger

29 GLOBE TROTTER

30 ORBIT.   (RETORTS) (ORBIT) LIBERTY)
$\quad\quad\quad\quad$ 2 5 1 $\quad$ 1 2 3 4 5 $\quad$ 4 3

31 mitre.   (It is headwear, the rest are worn on the feet.)

32 SQUASH

33 (e) a sheep

34 scale

35 A.

36 maw, stomach

37 OCCUPANT, RESIDENT

38 A HALF A LOAF IS BETTER THAN NONE BUT A WHOLE LOAF IS EVEN BETTER

39 ICE

40 Never. (At the fifth stage they return to their original positions and complete the loop, whereby they never visit the same corner together.)

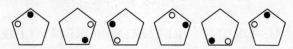

(Of course, two corners clockwise is exactly the same as three corners anticlockwise!)

41 GABRIELLE

42 meridian

43 56. $((10 - 7) \times 8 = 24, (9 - 5) \times 7 = 28, (11 - 4) \times 8 = 56)$

44 (b) a dingo

45 C. (The contents of columns 1 and 2 are added to give column 3. Similarly, the contents of rows 1 and 2 give row 3.)

46 ROMANTICALLY.
(The length of each word increases by two letters each time and commences with the middle two letters of the previous word.)

47 $4\frac{2}{3}$. $(\frac{7}{8} \times \frac{3}{4} \div \frac{1}{8} = \frac{7}{9} \times \frac{3}{4} \times \frac{8}{1} = \frac{168}{36} = \frac{14}{3} = 4\frac{2}{3})$

48 elegance

49 menace, impend

50 60. $(12 - 5 = 7, \times 5 = 35; 18 - 6 = 12, \times 11 = 132;$
$21 - 17 = 4, \times 13 = 52; 19 - 4 = 15, \times 4 = 60)$

Scoring Chart for Test 6

20–24	Average
25–29	Good
30–39	Very Good
40–44	Excellent
45–50	Exceptional

Test 7

1

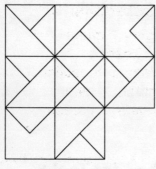

Find the missing tile from the options A to E below.

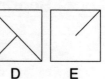

   A   B   C   D   E

2   Use every letter of the phrase below, once only, to spell out three girls' names.

AS A UNIVERSAL SON

3   Complete the five words below with the aid of the clues. Each word contains the same three letters which are represented by XYZ.

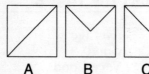

X Y Z _ _ _ _	Up-to-date.
_ X Y Z _ _ _	Ideally perfect.
_ _ X Y Z _ _	Mollusc.
_ _ _ X Y Z _	A form of an element.
_ _ _ _ X Y Z	Pinnacle.

122

4 Choose a pair of words, (a) to (e), that best expresses a relationship similar to the pair in capital letters.

SIMILE : COMPARISON

(a) metaphor : muse
(b) verb : speech
(c) tautology : repetition
(d) paragraph : letter
(e) alliteration : phrase

5 Which of the hexagons A to E is missing from the top of the pyramid?

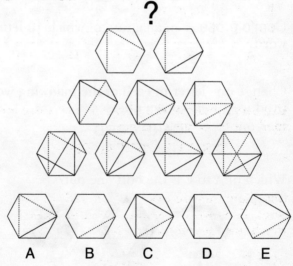

A   B   C   D   E

6 What phrase is suggested by the diagram? (3-6)
Clue: Hot season.

. . MM . .

7

8	23	3	49
19	4	29	17
37	25	35	16

In the array above, which of (a) to (e) below is the difference between the sum of the two highest prime numbers and the product of the two lowest square numbers?

(a) 0 (b) 1 (c) 2 (d) 4 (e) 12

8 Comic prose is an anagram of which 10-letter word?

9 Change one letter in each of the following words to produce a well-known phrase:

CAKE CARD

10 Which of A to E is the odd one out?

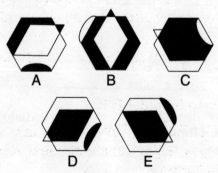

A   B   C

D   E

11 Complete the five words so that two letters are common to each word. That is, the same two letters that end the first word also start the second word, and so on. The two letters that end the fifth word are the first two letters of the first word, thus completing the circle.

```
_ _ I M _ _
_ _ L U _ _
_ _ B A _ _
_ _ R R _ _
_ _ P H _ _
```

12 Which two of these words are opposite in meaning?

smooth, evasive, shameful, noisy, candid, shunned

13 Fetch caesium is an an anagram of which familiar phrase? Clue: Boldly meet consequences.

14 Insert the word inside the brackets that has the same meaning as the definitions outside the brackets.

arrow case (. . . . . .) tremble

15 What is a brocade? Is it:

(a) a fortification (b) a badger lair
(c) heavy fabric (d) slender leaf stems
(e) Italian wine?

16

Which of the options below continues the above sequence?

A   B   C   D   E

17

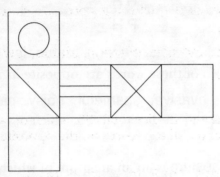

When the above is folded to form a cube, just one of A, B, C, D or E can be produced. Which one?

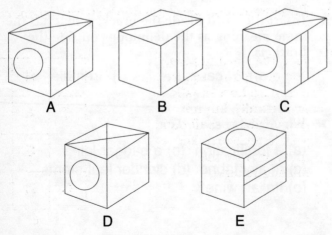

A   B   C

D   E

18 Complete the two words, one reading clockwise and the other reading anti-clockwise. One goes round the outer circle and the other round the inner circle. The two words are synonyms. You must provide the missing letters.

19 Which two of the following words are closest in meaning?

paragon, anomaly, criterion, statue, law, exigency

20 If the score of 12 dice totals 36, which of (a) – (e) is the average of the scores on the opposite sides?

(a) 2 (b) 3 (c) 4 (d) 5 (e) 6

21 Realigned is an anagram of which girl's name?

22 Find the starting point and move from square to square horizontally or vertically, but not diagonally, to spell out a 12-letter word. You must provide the missing letters.

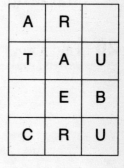

23 Which of A, B, C, D or E is the missing tile?

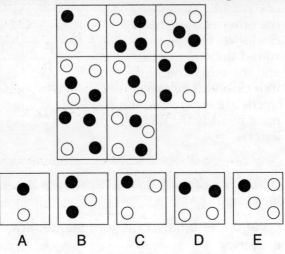

A   **B**   **C**   **D**   **E**

24   A B C D E F G H

Which letter is two the left of the letter three to the right of the letter immediately to the right of the letter three to the left of the letter G?

25 In a race of seven runners, in how many different ways can the first four places be filled?

(a) 22 (b) 24 (c) 210 (d) 840 (e) 2520

26 Find a word which, when placed in front of these words, makes new words.

$$(\_ \_ \_)$$

TABLE
BALL
MONEY
CUSHION
PRICK

27 Make a word. Clue: OUTRAGE.

L	I	N	V	E	C	O	E

28 Which of the following is not a hardwood?

maple, beech, spruce, elm, oak

29 Trace out a 10-letter word by travelling along the lines. Clue: REVENGEFUL.

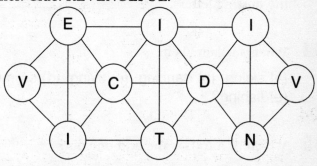

30 Which two of these words are similar in meaning?

parsimonious, dull, magnificent, prosaic, precocious, desirable

31   75632 : 75069 : 74563

Which three numbers below have the same relationship to one another as the three numbers above?

A	62195	:	61993	:	61845
B	28967	:	27878	:	26789
C	58213	:	57816	:	56382
D	99426	:	96514	:	94321
E	27316	:	26585	:	25927

32 Place a word inside the brackets which means the same as the two words outside the brackets.

seat (. . . . . .) establish

33 Start at one of the corner squares and move from square to square horizontally and vertically to spell out a 9-letter word. You must provide the missing letters.

I	L	
L	E	E
	I	G

34 What is volant? Is it:

(a) skiing (b) dancing (c) flying (d) swimming
(e) fishing?

35 Which of A to G is the odd one out?

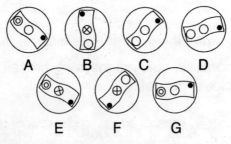

36 Which word inside the brackets is most opposite in meaning to the word in capital letters?

DISSOLUTE (acceptable, virtuous, collect, marry, purify)

37 Find the missing letters to make two 8-letter words which are synonyms. The words run clockwise.

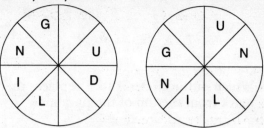

38 Find the saying. All of the vowels have been omitted and the word boundaries altered.

THGRS SLWYS SMSGR NRNTH THRMN SFLD

39 Find a word which, when placed in front of these words, makes new words.

FALL
BAG
(_ _ _ _)   PUMP
SOCK
TUNNEL

40 Place three of these 2-letter 'bits' together to make right hand.

DE, RI, ER, LE, XT, NT

41 What is a pharos? Is it:

(a) a monument (b) a sphinx (c) a liner
(d) an Egyptian statue (e) a lighthouse?

42 Which number should replace the question mark?

43 Which of the circles A to E replaces the question mark from the top of the pyramid?

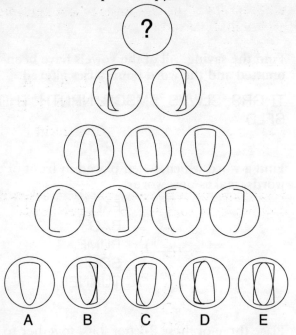

A   B   C   D   E

44 Find a one word anagram:

taste can

45 Select four of these five sets of a double letters to make wine merchants.

NR, NT, NE, VI, RS

46 Which number should replace the question mark?

9	8	7	2
11	5	9	4
8	5	7	3
12	4	4	?

47 With the aid of the clue, insert the letters into the grid to find the two words.

T L A L A
S R R Y E
Clue: lucid

48 What foodstuff is missing from the brackets reading downwards to complete the 3-letter words?

CO ( )
TO ( )
FO ( )
YO ( )
NO ( )
GO ( )

49 DHJ is to QUW as FIL is to which of these?

RWZ, SVY, PTX, ORV, RUY

50 Which word inside the brackets means the same as the word in capital letters?

RESILIENT (bold, springy, stiff, settled, demur)

1   E. (Looking both across and down, only lines common to the first two squares are carried forward to the third square.)

2   ALISON, SUSAN, VERA

3   topical, utopian, octopus, isotope, hilltop
(XYZ = TOP)

4   (c) tautology : repetition

5   D. (The contents of each hexagon are determined by the contents of the two hexagons below it. Only lines common to the two hexagons below are carried forward, with the added twist that two complete lines become dotted (or broken) and two broken lines become complete lines.)

6   MID-SUMMER

7   (c) 2.
(primes: 29 + 37 = 66;
  squares: 4 × 16 = 64.)

8   microscope

9   TAKE CARE

10 D. (A and C are the same figure, rotated, and with black and white reversed. B. and E are the same figure, rotated, and with black and white reversed.)

11 ANIMAL, ALLUDE, DEBATE, TERROR, ORPHAN

12 evasive, candid

13 Face the music

14 quiver

15 (c) heavy fabric

16 D. (The large arc rotates 90° clockwise; the middle arc rotates 45° anticlockwise; the small arc rotates 45° clockwise.)

17 A.

18 INTREPID, RESOLUTE

19 paragon, criterion

20 (c) 4. (Opposite sides of a die always total 7. On 12 dice, therefore, opposite faces total $12 \times 7 = 84$. As the totals on one side are 36, the totals on the opposite side are $84 - 36 = 48$. Dividing by 12 gives an average of 4.)

21 Geraldine

22 BUREAUCRATIC

23 C. (So that each horizontal and each vertical line contains 6 black and 6 white dots.)

24 F.

25 (d) 840. $(7 \times 6 \times 5 \times 4)$

26 PIN

27 VIOLENCE

28 spruce

29 VINDICTIVE

30 prosaic, dull

31 E. 27316 : 26585 : 25927.
(Take the number formed by the middle three digits of the previous number and deduct: $27316 - 731 = 26585$. $26585 - 658 = 25927$.)

32 settle

33 ILLEGIBLE

34 (c) flying

35 E. (A is the same as G but rotated. B is the same as
F but rotated. C is the same as D but rotated.)

36 virtuous

37 MUDDLING, BUNGLING

38 THE GRASS ALWAYS SEEMS GREENER IN THE
OTHER MAN'S FIELD.

39 WIND

40 DEXTER

41 (e) a lighthouse

42 312. ((9 + 1 + 7) × (3 × 2 × 1) = 102;
(8 + 3 + 5) × (2 × 2 × 3) = 192;
(7 + 2 + 4) × (3 × 2 × 4) = 312)

43 E. (The contents of each circle are determined by
the contents of the two circles immediately
below it. These combine, but symbols which are
the same disappear.)

44 castanet

45 VINTNERS

46 4. (9 + 7 = 16, ÷ 8 = 2
         11 + 9 = 20, ÷ 5 = 4
          8 + 7 = 15, ÷ 5 = 3
         12 + 4 = 16, ÷ 4 = 4)

47 CRYSTAL CLEAR

48 YOGURT (To give COY, TOO, FOG, YOU, NOR, GOT.)

49 SVY. (These letters occupy the same position in the second half of the alphabet as FIL in the first half:
A B C D E F G H I J K L M
N O P Q R S T U V W X Y Z

50 springy

Scoring Chart for Test 7

20–24	Average
25–29	Good
30–39	Very Good
40–44	Excellent
45–50	Exceptional

Test 8

1   Which three of these four pieces can be fitted together to form a square? Choose from options A, B or C.

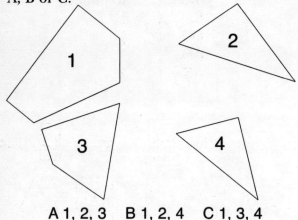

A 1, 2, 3   B 1, 2, 4   C 1, 3, 4

2   Complete the two words, one reading clockwise and the other reading anticlockwise. One is found round the outer circle and the other round the inner circle. The two words are synonyms. You must provide the missing letters.

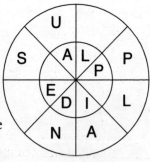

3   What is sternutation? Is it:

(a) heavy breathing (b) the act of sneezing
(c) shouting loudly (d) a strict upbringing
(e) bringing up the rear?

4 The name of which Shakespeare character can be placed in the brackets reading downwards to complete the 3-letter words.

$$
\begin{array}{ll}
\text{WA} & (\quad) \\
\text{AS} & (\quad) \\
\text{MA} & (\quad) \\
\text{IL} & (\quad) \\
\text{DU} & (\quad) \\
\text{AR} & (\quad) \\
\text{AS} & (\quad) \\
\end{array}
$$

5

□△△□ is to [⊙] as △○△ is to:

A   B   C   D   E

6 Place three of these 2-letter 'bits' together to make vibrate.

SH, ER, HO, JU, UD, DD

7 Find the starting point and move from square to square horizontally or vertically, but not diagonally, to spell out a 12-letter word. You must provide the missing letters.

T	A	L
N	E	
	P	I
E	E	R

141

8

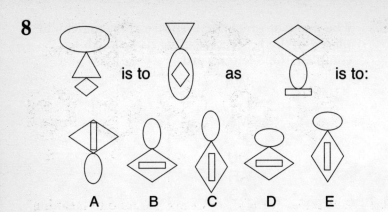

is to as is to:

A   B   C   D   E

9   **Begot this queen** is an anagram of which phrase?
(3, 3, 8) Clue: Polite request.

10 Which word is indicated in the diagram?

> **G**
> **N**

11 Place two letters in each set of brackets so that they
finish the word on the left and start the word on
the right. You must choose the correct letters so
that when read in pairs, downwards, they will spell
out an eight-letter word.

NE (. .) EW
SP (. .) GE
CA (. .) AR
NO (. .) CE

12 What word goes after all of the following to make
five new words?

A, IN, CO, TO, S

13

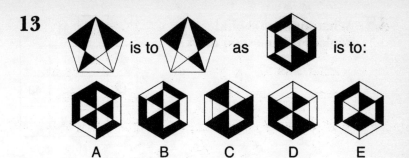

is to   as   is to:

A   B   C   D   E

14 Which two of these words are opposite in meaning?

wistful, loved, wrathful, forceful, mindful, contented

15 What is the longest word that can be produced from the letters below, using each letter only once?

K E N T S O U B A R

16   IMPS   (OPTIMISM)   OMIT
              ?   (CONTRIVE)   VICE

Which of the words (a) to (e) should replace the question mark?

(a) NOTE (b) TORN (c) IRON (d) CENT
(e) NICE

17 Which of these is not an anagram of a precious stone?

(a)   MAD LEER
(b)   SO SCAMP
(c)   ARGENT
(d)   MET HASTY
(e)   HIS PAPER

18 What number should replace the question mark?

		31	
	22		
13			43
		?	

19 In each team of 30 players in a game that lasts for 24 minutes, there are six reserves. The reserves alternate equally with each player. Therefore, all 36 players are on the pitch for the same length of time. For how long?

20

Which of the options A – E comes next?

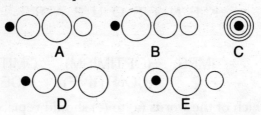

21 Choose a pair of words, (a) to (e), that best expresses a relationship similar to the pair in capital letters.

	FORMAL	:	RELAXED
(a)	cynical	:	quizzical
(b)	pleased	:	enthusiastic
(c)	sceptical	:	credulous
(d)	scribble	:	paint
(e)	forfeit	:	disallow

22 Which of these is the odd one out?

formidable, considerable, redoubtable, momentous, prominent

23 Which of these is not an anagram of a country?

     (a)   AND GLEN
     (b)   OR YAWN
     (c)   OLD PAN
     (d)   LET CAR
     (e)   CAR FEN

24 Complete the five words so that two letters are common to each word. That is, the same two letters that end the first word also start the second word, and so on. The two letters that end the fifth word are the first two letters of the first word, thus completing the circle.

```
_ _ I T _ _
_ _ N A _ _
_ _ M P _ _
_ _ T H _ _
_ _ L I _ _
```

25 Change one letter only in each of the following words to produce a well known phrase:

SPAN I WARN

26 Place a word within the brackets which means the same as the words outside the brackets.

surprise (. . . . .) shaggy hair

27 Trace out a 10-letter word by travelling along the lines. Clue: TRAVELLERS.

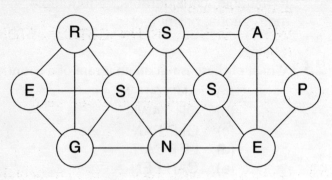

28 Find a word which, when placed in front of these words, makes new words.

(_ _ _ _ _)

EYED
PATCH
STITCH
LEGGED
BENCH

29 Make a word. Clue: REPRIMANDS.

C	U	T	L	E	R	S	E

30 Which two of these words are similar in meaning?

embroil, gregarious, nebulous, prim, confuse, degenerate

31 Find the amusing variation of a well-known saying. The vowels have been omitted and the word boundaries changed.

VRYCL DHSSL VRLNN GBTSM JSTBR NGRN

32 Which letter should logically follow next?

A, F, H, K, N, ? ,

33 Find a word which, when placed in front of these words, makes new words.

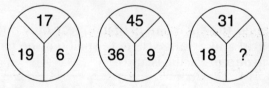

(_ _ _)   STOP
TED
FALL
PONY
BATH

34 What is the missing number?

17
19 | 6

45
36 | 9

31
18 | ?

35 rag, object, yachts, gamut, ? , intend, vacuum

What word is missing from the above list? Choose from:

beast, four, bait, charm, endure

36 Each of the nine squares in the grid marked 1A to 3C, should incorporate all the lines and symbols which are shown in the squares of the same letter and number immediately above and to the left. For example, 2B should incorporate all the lines and symbols that are in 2 and B.

   One of the squares is incorrect. Which one is it?

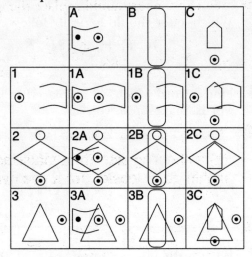

37 Find the eight letters that appear only once in the grid and arrange them to spell out the name of a group of Pacific islands.

U	G	J	U	Q	I	V
X	F	O	B	D	K	C
N	M	L	Q	Y	H	P
W	K	S	F	T	R	B
G	J	C	H	K	X	E
A	R	T	V	W	M	D

38

25	(149)	97
31	(611)	58
29	(?)	64

What number is missing above?

39 Which number should replace the question mark?

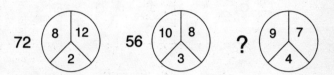

40 What is a nereid? Is it:

(a) a shooting star (b) a magician (c) a sea urchin (d) a lobster (e) a sea nymph?

41

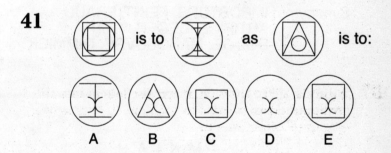

42 Find a one-word anagram:

leap bay

43 What is oviferous? Is it:

(a) oval shaped (b) outspoken (c) parchment (d) hexagonal (e) egg-bearing?

44 Find the missing letters to make two words which are synonyms. The words may run either clockwise or anticlockwise.

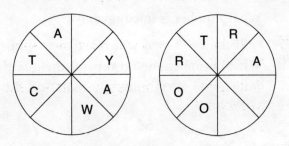

45   Keyword: TRICK

Nine synonyms of the above keyword are listed. Take one letter from each to find a further synonym of the keyword. The letters appear in the correct order.

Synonyms: IMPOSTURE, FEINT, FRAUD,
          ARTIFICE, DECEIT, TRAP,
          DODGE, MANOEUVRE, GIMMICK

46 With the aid of the clue, insert the letters into the grid to find two words.

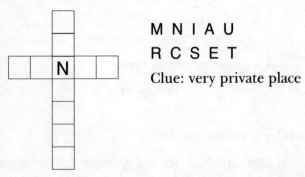

M N I A U
R C S E T
Clue: very private place

150

47 Select four of the five sets of double letters and arrange them to make an advance party.

RD, NG, UE, UA, VA

48 Find the two words which are most similar in meaning.

deity, sybil, prophetess, sepulchre, rhombic, sycophant

49 Which number should replace the question mark?

17	3	14	9
16	4	12	16
18	4	9	36
27	2	3	?

50 What is a brouhaha? Is it:

(a) a conference (b) a vegetable (c) a tumult
(d) a bird (e) a fish?

Answers Test 8

1   C 1, 3, 4.

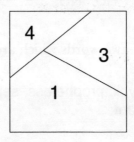

2   SUPPLANT, DISPLACE

3   (b) the act of sneezing

4   SHYLOCK (To give WAS, ASH, MAY, ILL, DUO, ARC, ASK.)

5   E. (The rectangle turns through 90° and the circle inside it changes to a triangle. The figures either side (the triangles) turn into one large triangle which surrounds the rectangle.)

6   JUDDER

7   EXPERIMENTAL

8   C. (The shape at the top rotates through 90° and goes to the bottom. The shape at the bottom rotates through 90° and goes in the shape previously at the top. The shape in the middle rotates through 180° and goes to the top.)

9   Beg the question

10   GOVERN.   (G over N)

11   STURGEON

12   WARD

13   B. (It is a mirror image of the original.)

14   wrathful, contented

15   OUTBREAKS

16   (b) TORN.   (TORN/VICE is an anagram of CONTRIVE.)

17   (b) SO SCAMP = compass.
      (MAD LEER = emerald; ARGENT = garnet; MET HASTY = amethyst; HIS PAPER = sapphire.)

18   34. (Each number describes its position in the grid. Thus, 34 = 3 lines across, 4 lines down.)

19   20 minutes. $((24 \times 30) \div 36)$

20 A. (The smallest white circle moves from left to
right, one circle at a time, at each stage. The
black dot similarly moves from right to left.)

21 (c) sceptical : credulous

22 considerable

23 (d) LET CAR = cartel or claret
(AND GLEN = England; OR YAWN =
Norway; OLD PAN = Poland; CAR FEN =
France.)

24 EDITOR, ORNATE, TEMPLE, LETHAL, ALLIED

25 SPIN A YARN

26 shock

27 PASSENGERS

28 CROSS

29 LECTURES

30 embroil, confuse

31 EVERY CLOUD HAS A SILVER LINING BUT SOME JUST BRING RAIN

32 Y. (All letters are made up of three straight lines.)

33 PIT

34 7. (17 + 19 = 36, square root = 6;
45 + 36 = 81, square root = 9;
31 + 18 = 49, square root = 7)

35 bait (Each word begins with the initial letter of the seven colours of the rainbow, in order: red, orange, yellow, green, blue, indigo, violet, and is the same number of letters long as is the colour.)

36 1A.

37 POLYNESIA

38 156. (5 + 9 = 14, 2 + 7 = 9; 1 + 5 = 6, 3 + 8 = 11; 9 + 6 = 15, 2 + 4 = 6)

39 35. ((8 – 2) × 12 = 72, (10 – 3) × 8 = 56, (9 – 4) × 7 = 35)

40 (e) a sea nymph

41 A. (The circle opens and reverses. The vertical sides of the square slide in. The triangle sides slide in.)

42 payable

43 (e) egg-bearing

44 HATCHWAY, TRAPDOOR

45 STRATAGEM

46 INNER SANCTUM

47 VANGUARD

48 sybil, prophetess

49 48. (17 − 14 = 3, × 3 = 9
     16 − 12 = 4, × 4 = 16
     18 − 9 = 9, × 4 = 36
     27 − 3 = 24, × 2 = 48)

50 (c) a tumult

Scoring Chart for Test 8

20–24	Average
25–29	Good
30–39	Very Good
40–44	Excellent
45–50	Exceptional

Total scoring chart for the eight tests

160–199   Average
200–239   Good
240–319   Very Good
320–359   Excellent
360–400   Exceptional